The Participant Self

The
Participant
Self

Adrian van Kaam

Bert van Croonenburg

Susan Muto

DIMENSION BOOKS, INC.

Denville, New Jersey

First American Edition

PUBLISHED BY DIMENSION BOOKS

DENVILLE, NEW JERSEY

Library of Congress Catalog Card Number 71-106896

Copyright © 1969 by Dimension Books, Inc.

Book I

The Participant Self
is a sequel to
The Emergent Self

TABLE OF CONTENTS

PREFACE

In days gone by no man could avoid participation.

To refuse cooperation was to be cast out of tribe or camp, to risk enslavement by a hostile clan.

* * *

Villagers toiled together in field and forest, shop and home with tools handmade from stone and timber.

The fabrics of dress and shelter, the fare spread sparsely or profusely, participated in the stirring life of field and forest, stream and sky.

* * *

Eating, dressing, drinking, dwelling entwined self with neighbor and nature.

Farmers, hunters, fishermen, bakers, butchers, weavers, struggled side by side, blending resources, strength and skills.

* * *

While eating the bread of the baker, while wearing the cloak of the weaver, each man, woman and child shared in the life and labor of those he knew as craftsman, neighbor, friend.

* * *

Each laborer was a living sign of a lively tradition of coping with the challenge of rock and river, sod and swamp.

Community and its sacred history stood revealed in labors visible to all from childhood on.

* * *

Ceremonies and celebrations bound every task to the mystery that encompassed and sustained the common life.

No matter what man did in hamlet or home, his was a religious participation in the whole that surpasses all.

* * *

Man's longing for participation was fostered and fulfilled.

His life was full of meaning. He was at home in cosmos and community.

* * *

Time passed. Village faded into town, town into city, city into suburbia.

Suburbia may be a pattern of immaculate streets, a collection of lonely houses strung like beads on clean winding cords.

Suburbia: a sometimes silent monument to the remains of human participation.

Life seems buried under layers of mixed cement and mown grass.

Commuters travel to office and factory far away.

Returning by train and car, they retire to island homes afloat in lakes of green. There they remain, smiling strangers to one another.

* * *

Food, dress, furniture, supplies, produced and packaged by men and machines in automated mills, are shipped by truck and train, boat and plane piloted by strangers.

* * *

Dependence on family, friend and neighbor may become a vestige of the past.

Functionaries and computers may shelter, nourish and attire all.

The ill and disabled may no longer be invitations to leave our fortress of good fortune for a moment of compassion.

* * *

Only a fraction of his time, increasingly small, shall the man of tomorrow spend in common labor.

His position in the chain of performance and production will be more and more anonymous, his activity attuned to the stacatto rhythm of key punch and computer.

* * *

While personal engagement is difficult to maintain and may be more so in days to come, without participation man loses his humanity.

* * *

Compassion and concern initiated in situations adverse to their emergence may gain in depth and meaning.

* * *

Intimacy imposed by fate or tribal necessity can be stifling and oppressive.

* * *

In the past participation was often unfree, forcing intimacy even when there was no spontaneous affinity.

For survival's sake men were compelled to accommodate each other often at the cost of personal unfolding.

16

Compulsive companionship could suffocate the emergence of personality.

* * *

Forms of free participation must be found, enabling us to cultivate our humanity, even when not engaged intimately.

* * *

To freely seek and find intimates with whom I feel affinity, enables me to be and become who I am.

In choosing my friends, I choose myself.

* * *

Loss of intimacy with all does not mean loss of all intimacy.

* * *

Intimate involvement with all is unfeasible.

To strive for respectful presence to all is commendable.

* * *

That forced intimacy between neighbors disappeared is a momentous gain in the history of human dignity.

Participation, once an imposed necessity, has become an art of sharing and an attitude of listening to nuances which challenge us continually.

I

COMMUNION

In what sense is communion a profound expression of participation?

When my eyes meet the eyes of a peaceful man, I may share his serenity.

When a child brushes the tears from his cheek, I may feel a dampness on mine.

I am alive to what we are and in the deepest sense we are in communion.

* * *

No child is born who is not in communion with all children.

No man dies who does not die with others.

No person worships alone. His prayer is shared by countless others in crowded cities and quiet homes.

In birth, death and prayer, in laughter and lamentation, I am an act of sharing. I am not only in communion, I am communion.

* * *

If I laugh, others, near and far, are laughing with me. If I cry, tears are being shed in hovels and homes whose doorsteps I may never cross.

* * *

Human experience is participation in the life of every person who has ever lived.

I step across the threshold of loneliness into communion with those who are, were, and may yet be.

* * *

In communion I am immersed in the waves of a humanity which recurrently loses and finds itself.

I feel nostalgia for what was and is no more. At the same time, in tending toward the future, I give voice to the moment which is my own.

* * *

Communion with others begins when I come into union with self in solitude.

* * *

My search for self may disclose not only the me of light and laughter but the me of darkness and tears.

I reach out and find a person who is not only a search for goodness, truth and beauty but also one beset by envy, jealousy and greed.

* * *

I may climb to the top of the mountain and inhale the good, sweet air of wisdom and love, yet before I know it, I am cascading like a waterfall into the valley below.

* * *

If I hide from myself my propensity for power, I may never meet a person as he is.

I may force him to be someone he is not or fail to forgive him when he strays from patterns of life I have impressed on him.

* * *

Communion with the needs of others may excite my generosity and fire my imagination.

My eagerness should be balanced by candid appraisal of my needs, limitations, and interests.

24

* * *

A service to which I am not called by talent and temperament but by contagious enthusiasm may be a disservice to humanity.

* * *

Communion extends beyond time and place. It is an invitation to commune with all that is, a homecoming that brings harmony to my life.

* * *

The communion I am is the communion which binds all things.

Just as each petal of a rose melts into the fullness of its perfection, so each event of life weaves itself into every other forming a vibrant whole.

The harmony of life goes deeper than its disruptions.

* * *

In moments of meditative presence communion may become consecration: I abide in my deepest self where the Holy invites me to see in His Light all that I am and encounter.

* * *

In prayer I feel that I am in the world but not of the world.

In no way do I escape my humanness; in no way do I distance myself from our common concern.

Rather, in piercing to the depths of our world, I discover what binds us together.

II

RETREAT

Does communion mean we must always be together? Is there no room for retreat?

Communion is unreachable without retreat.

The call to retreat reminds me to return to myself and reconfirm my personal dignity. The call to communion opens me to the possibility of affirming others and being affirmed by them.

* * *

A child may retreat from an animal that frightens him.

A warrior may retreat to mislead an invader.

A monk may retreat to live the life of the spirit.

30

These times of retreat reveal man's ability to distance himself when necessary.

* * *

At times I must leave the world of people and appointments to refind my reason for living.

While ways of retreat differ from person to person, abiding in solitude is as beneficial as communing with others.

There is a time for withholding and a time for participating, a time to preserve privacy, a time to welcome intimacy.

* * *

Retreat is not a flight from life but a journey to its depth.

* * *

A fortunate man, gifted with a lovely family and the benefits of an affluent society, may awaken one morning and ask, "What is the meaning of it all?"

This question is a call to retreat.

* * *

In retreat a horizon appears against which disparate experiences gain perspective.

* * *

Love gathers new meanings in retreat. It is no longer taken for granted.

* * *

In retreat from accomplishment and acquisition, I may center the meaning of prosperity in personal values.

I recall that success as such does not really matter. What counts is how sincerely I have tried to live those values that bring worth to human life.

* * *

What is called retreat may be a way of closing myself off from life's demands.

I refuse to see ills which beg to be cured or lives which ask to be saved.

* * *

False retreat can be escape into the complacency of common consciousness.

Here I become an anonymous me, a marionette who assumes no responsibility for my life or for the lives of those entrusted to my care.

* * *

To evade the invitation to be what I am

32

is tempting in an age which derides uniqueness and exalts uniformity.

Flight into common consciousness offers
release from the summons of self.

* * *

Withdrawal from self can mean absorp-
tion in a movement, crusade or cause.

The moment of total immersion is often
the moment of total escape.

* * *

When I retire inwardly, I may sense what
moves me to action.

I may find that the person I am running
away from most is myself.

* * *

The more passionately I participate in generous plans and projects, the more they
empty me out if I never retreat to preserve
my privacy.

* * *

In a public world privacy becomes ever
more precious.

The more difficult it is to retreat outward-
ly, the more pressing is the need to retreat
inwardly.

33

* * *

There are moments when I must be alone, when the intensity of my experience can be shared with no one.

What is called concern may then be an invasion of privacy.

* * *

Growing respect for my right to solitude insures that I shall grant the other his time and place of retreat.

* * *

Retreat sustains my attempt to survive not only as a manager but also as a man.

* * *

Integration of life is an ongoing endeavor, brought closer to culmination by timely retreat to the origins of my participating self.

III

LABOR

Separation of life and labor seems to plague modern man. Is there a way to overcome this cleavage?

The I who laughs and loves and plays should be the I who works.

* * *

Choosing one kind of work rather than another is not simply a result of education.

My preference is also an expression of inspiration, temperament and disposition.

* * *

If I tend to be reflective, I may find that the labor I enjoy involves thinking, reading, writing or aesthetic creation.

If I am more inclined to be active and outgoing, I may participate in projects of welfare and social change.

38

If my penchant is for sports and exercise, my favorite work may range from manual labor to mountain climbing.

*   *   *

Without a creative approach, labor loses inspiration.

The uncreative laborer sees the world as a dead, routinized place offering him a limited number of things to do.

He has to expend energy to fight off boredom and quell the restlessness of his original self.

*   *   *

The creative laborer experiences his surroundings as a field of infinite invitation.

*   *   *

The uncreative teacher sees only the same classroom, the same faces, the same grades and meetings.

Teaching for him is a passing on of information from year to year; he may know what his students have learned but not who they are.

*   *   *

39

The creative teacher appeals to the unique potential of every pupil.

His teaching radiates personal value which he communicates by word, gesture, deed.

What he imparts is not a collection of data but communion with wisdom, the meaning every moment of life may reveal.

* * *

A good nurse lives the union of life and labor. Unlike the nurse who is more a dispensing machine than a person, she listens to her patient, easing apprehension and distress.

Her caring presence weaves an atmosphere of trust that lingers long after she leaves.

* * *

When labor is separated from life, I may compartmentalize my day into hours when I earn my living and hours when I attempt to live.

When living is divorced from doing, both are diminished. Action is strained and emotion frustrated.

* * *

When most of my day is spent in an un-bending mood of getting things done, it is difficult to switch to the warmth and ease of an evening at home.

* * *

The strain of impersonal productivity be-gins to tell in the way I speak and move.

Rigidity sets in. My gestures become less graceful. An ordering domineering tone creeps into my voice.

The other may feel that I am using him as a pawn in a business venture, that I pre-tend concern to secure compliance and cooperation.

* * *

Labor may become an exercise in efficien-cy, a means to gain power and profit, stunt-ing my growth in generosity.

* * *

Without foregoing profit and productiv-ity, labor can be an avenue to personal growth, involving enjoyment, service to hu-manity, generous dedication to an ennobling cause.

* * *

41

Perceiving the deeper meaning of what I do may not change the task itself; it does change my attitude toward labor, bringing it closer to my life.

* * *

When labor becomes a burden only, I will dread each day on the job, restlessly waiting for the end of the week to come.

A weekend cannot cure the bitterness of a week nor can two weeks vacation redeem a year's loss of life.

* * *

If I work and never pause to ask, "What for?", I may become an expert in the creation of means, not daring to ponder the end of my actions.

Accumulating means without ends is a demeaning activity.

* * *

Gratification through work is not assured by inner attitude alone.

Though labor entails drudgery and routine, it should never be so routinized that it cannot instill moments of joy.

* * *

When people believe that labor is merely a burden to be borne, there will be little research and action to heal the rift between life and labor for those who cannot cure this wound themselves.

*   *   *

It is mankind's sacred duty to diminish the hours of drudgery that form an unavoidable part of every working day.

*   *   *

Though I may have convinced myself that work and play, toil and contentment, labor and leisure do not belong together, they are inseparable.

The productive I and the creative I are conjoined in every human endeavor.

Life becomes more worthwhile when labor is the incarnation of my whole, loving, joyful, warm and spontaneous self.

IV

LEISURE

What bearing does leisure have on life and labor?

Life enslaved by labor may suffocate me in a viselike hold which reaches beyond working hours.

Labor may so override me that when I fall ill my first thought is likely to be: "What about all the things left undone?"

* * *

I may have paid too high a price for the security my position brings.

Gone is my creativity, dessicated my spontaneity, forgotten my desire to soar beyond the tyranny of the now.

Though this desire may be denied, it cannot be destroyed without suffering disharmony.

48

* * *

Leisure humanizes labor, freeing me from preoccupation with power, status and possession.

* * *

Without leisure, I may be confined to useful time alone, where hours are computed thriftily in terms of tasks to be performed and profits to be made.

* * *

Leisure is to dwell unhurriedly in the timelessness of useless presence to world, self and others.

* * *

Leisure yokes the timeless and the temporal.

The incongruity of human events, the endless paradoxes and contradictions — all fall into place.

In this liberated mood life decisions may be made.

* * *

Living in leisure reveals the truth of what it is to be man and to be part of something that is more than man in isolation.

In moments of leisure, I may forget the dictates of time and open up to the eternal.

* * *

Leisure is the root of contemplation. Beyond the pressures of daily duty, I am invited to participate in what is festive and sacred in life and world.

* * *

Play and celebration are spontaneous expressions of the leisurely attitude.

* * *

Letting go, and letting life in, is play.

* * *

Look at the child. For him there is no time in play; space is the piece of earth that supports his game.

A sense of wonder transforms the commonplace. A simple room becomes a palace in which he reigns as king.

A child can play the same game, discovering something new each time the rhyme is repeated or the mulberry bush is gone 'round.

* * *

Potentialities I never knew I possessed

may come to light in play.

New regions of enjoyment and action open before me.

*　*　*

Involved in playful action, I may remain purposeful, ready to illumine my task with the light that emerges in aimless play.

Involved in purposeful action, I may remain pliant and playful, ready to receive new insight that wells up from labor to which I bring love and concern.

*　*　*

The game, dance, song, the play of love carry me beyond self to a sense of wholeness easily lost in fragmented performance.

*　*　*

Leisurely acceptance of life discloses meanings which defy attempts at mastery.

Like prayer, play allows me to leave the world of useful time, where every second counts. Life is lived as an embodiment of love freely given and freely received.

V

EXPERIENCE

How can I expand and deepen my experience without losing inner harmony.?

Reading a line of poetry may touch a chord of truth. Something resonates in me.

What I read is felt personally.

Experience is happening to me.

* * *

On a summer day I may feel the warmth of the sun on my face, smell the grass under my feet, lose myself looking at the shimmering leaves of an ancient tree.

I am alive to the beauty of nature.

Experience is happening to me.

* * *

When I mourn my beloved, cringe with

pain, feel the betrayal of those I trusted, I am touched by tragedy.

Experience is happening to me.

* * *

What I have read, what I have felt, what I have suffered can become mine.

When this happens, life is enriched.

* * *

The depth and range of my experience depends on the way in which I am present to life.

If I approach life in a onesided or superficial manner, truths waiting to impress themselves upon me may escape me.

* * *

To experience life as it is, I must purify my outlook and expand my points of view.

This is possible when I do not catalogue experience in light of inflexible categories nor content myself with a shallow fleeting attention.

* * *

Man cannot widen his vision without widening his experience nor deepen his experience without deepening his presence.

* * *

At times the world appears a friendly place which calls me home. At times it seems a wilderness leaving me forlorn and alone.

Each experience can be worthwhile.

The world as home may replenish my tenderness. The world as wilderness may restore my strength.

* * *

Ambiguity, paradox and uncertainty brighten and obscure the experience of man.

Elegance and cruelty merge in the fight of the matador.

Exhaustion and elation mingle at the end of a well run race.

An ugly woman may look beautiful to a loving man.

* * *

Experience may be cursory, fast and fleeting, neither dwelling nor abiding.

My life may be like that of a man on a fast-moving train who never sees the countryside, only a blur of brown-green licking the sash of his compartment window.

58

There is no time to see the beauty of a tree, the brightness of a flower.

People and places melt together; faces become one face which is really no face, a mere faceless mask, an empty shell.

* * *

I may overcome apathy by sharing the cheer and gloom, faith and frustration of those with whom I live and labor.

Responding to the joy and sorrow of a shared present, we invite each other to participate in vivid experiences emerging in our lives together.

* * *

Experience is an adventure in change and adaptation.

I must dwell on experience quietly to assimilate it harmoniously into my life.

Assimilation never ends. Each experience initiates a new search for dynamic value.

* * *

I am always reaching beyond the limits of life to the experience of happiness without end, beauty without flaw, love without infidelity, joy without affliction.

59

I am always reaching for the absolute yet failing to attain it.

* * *

In daily life I experience myself as a tension between freedom and restraint.

I would like to realize dreams and ideals but feel impeded by the boundaries of history, the conditions of my body, the confines of my surroundings.

Limitation is no cause for despair but an invitation to respond creatively to the freedom in bondage which I am.

* * *

The summit of response to life may be reached at the moment I am most myself and most not myself, most assertive and most receptive.

* * *

It is consoling to know that I may find peace in the experience of self as carried by the Sacred through a range of adventures toward a final moment of resolution.

VI

EVALUATION

Human life unfolds itself in experience. How can each experience become truly mine?

Evaluation clarifies experience, drawing it into the totality of life's meaning.

* * *

Initially I may have known something was worthwhile without being able to appreciate its full meaning for me.

* * *

Evaluation of experience may reveal that I am fighting myself for the sake of adapting to trends of the times.

I may swing from one fad to another, never stopping to ask if it helps me personally or plunges me into the passing stream of whim and fashion.

* * *

As a prisoner of the fashionable world, I no longer value experience in light of the emerging style of my life.

* * *

In an age which values means more than ends, the temptation is not to ask what for, but to idolize means as values in themselves.

When means are idolized, when technique becomes its own end, I may pass responsibility to crowd or collectivity.

If the crowd does my thinking for me, I am already absorbed in anonymity.

No longer knowing how I feel may quench the springs of creative response. Like a parasite I live on the response of others.

* * *

Can I reaffirm values regarded as obsolete? Can I say yes to what is valuable in spite of its unpopularity?

* * *

Every value needs a witness.

A world filled with noise needs persons who dwell in solitude.

Painters and poets must arise to serve man's openness for beauty.

Societies, forgetful of human suffering, must be reminded of compassion by those who live lives of social dedication.

Inspired by witnesses for value, we may participate in the experience of meeting the sacred, of building community, of sensing the symbolic.

* * *

I share a world with others and must learn to live with their insights, even though I cannot value them personally.

* * *

Only when I have the courage to reaffirm what life means to me can I be myself and give substance to my belief.

* * *

If my self esteem is too high, I am bound to fail in an attempt to live ideals beyond me.

If I esteem others too highly, I risk the possibility of the pedestal falling down.

* * *

I may depreciate values I myself am unable to live. Devaluation then falsifies my sense of values.

* * *

It may be difficult to admit that something is worthwhile when I know it cannot be mine.

The valuable remains enjoyable even without the joy of possession.

* * *

Painful is the loss of value that would have been mine had I been faithful to its invitation.

The burden of guilt about values betrayed may lead me to deny what is lastingly valuable.

* * *

Devaluation distorts experience. Judgments become untrustworthy. Resentment overwhelms me when I meet a person whose values I cannot attain.

* * *

Devaluation reverses the order of values.

Vexed by originality I exalt conformity. Fearful of tenderness, I extol virility. Suspicious of authority, I foment anarchy.

67

* * *

Denial of value is a denial of humanity.

The true order of value offers itself only to those who welcome the message of truth and beauty no matter from whence it comes.

VII

PARTICIPATION

How can I find and follow the path of participation?

Participation is sharing in the unfolding of man and world.

* * *

Unlike mere service, service inspired by participation touches the inner fibers of person and society.

* * *

Whether participation is social, aesthetic or religious, each activity carries the imprint of my unique approach. Existing patterns are invitations to playful reflection, not closed doors preventing new proposals.

* * *

My personal choice of participation is one among many.

A manual laborer participates in the culture with his working hands, a pianist with his playing hands, a mother with her caring hands.

Different, yet alike, all speak of care and humanize the world.

* * *

Participation without recollection can destroy me as a person.

The rhythm of participation and recollection is like listening to life before speaking, pondering before acting, plowing before sowing.

While I may flee from solitude to action, only in the blending of both is human life enhanced.

* * *

When I listen to life in solitude, it does not disclose empty clichés but the wisdom of generations which intimates secrets of living I cannot decipher alone.

* * *

Dialogue with men of vision deepens appreciation of life and avails me of more than passing needs and ephemeral views.

*   *   *

To ease human deprivation I must be there in my uniqueness, finding my way to serve affluent or indigent without succumbing to the way of others which may not be right for me.

Participation is being myself, not being a pendant of the community.

*   *   *

Others may grant me the possibility of finding myself but they cannot live my life for me.

I am in the world as my own responsibility.

*   *   *

Only when we listen to one another can we reach sincere respect in spite of opposing views and unpleasant traits.

The path is then open to true participation.

*   *   *

Participation may be a prelude to self emergence through others.

Do I sustain those who are working with me to unfold the culture? Do I see myself as far from being the final judge of their words and actions?

Sensitive answers to such self-searching questions announce the dawning of a new age of participation.